THE CAUSES OF

SCHOOL VIOLENCE

Essential Viewpoints

THE CAUSES OF SCHOOL VIOLENCE

BY HELGA SCHIER

Content Consultant
Professor James Garbarino, Ph.D.
Maude C. Clarke Chair in Humanistic Psychology

ABDO
Publishing Company

CREDITS

Published by ABDO Publishing Company, 8000 West 78th Street, Edina, Minnesota 55439. Copyright © 2008 by Abdo Consulting Group, Inc. International copyrights reserved in all countries. No part of this book may be reproduced in any form without written permission from the publisher. The Essential Library™ is a trademark and logo of ABDO Publishing Company.

Printed in the United States.

Editor: Patricia Stockland
Copy Editor: Paula Lewis
Interior Design and Production: Emily Love
Cover Design: Emily Love

Library of Congress Cataloging-in-Publication Data
Schier, Helga.
  The causes of school violence / Helga Schier.
    p. cm. — (Essential viewpoints)
  Includes bibliographical references and index.
  ISBN 978-1-60453-060-5
  1. School violence—United States. I. Title.

  LB3013.3.S345 2008
  371.7'82—dc22

                              2007031920

TABLE OF CONTENTS

A typical classroom in the United States

How Much Violence Occurs?

he National Center for Education Statistics of the U.S. Department of Education reports that during the 2004–2005 school year, 28 students between the ages of five and 18 were victims of school-associated violent deaths.

Despite the sensational reports of fatal gunshots on some campuses, serious violent crimes are rare at school. However, the Goal 7 of *Goals 2000: Educate America Act* from 1994 still had not been met. This act proclaimed:

> *By the year 2000, every school in the United States will be free of drugs, violence, and the unauthorized presence of firearms and alcohol and will offer a disciplined environment conducive to learning.*[1]

In the 2003–2004 school year, 96 percent of high schools, 94 percent of middle schools, and 74 percent of elementary schools reported violent incidents of crime. Serious violent crime may not be a daily occurrence at most U.S. schools, but American schools are not free of crime and violence either.

Extreme examples such as school shootings are just a small part of the overall problem of school violence. However, they still make an impact on greater society. Every time a gun is fired on school property, the belief in the safety of American

Victims of Violence

The Constitutional Rights Foundation reports, "Every year, 3 million young people in the United States fall victim to crimes at school. Almost 2 million of these incidents involve violence."[2] Very few of the students causing this violence are the students who commit school shootings.

schools receives a blow. Students, parents, educators, lawmakers, the police, and politicians continuously seek answers to the question: how could this happen?

SEARCHING FOR ANSWERS AND TAKING SIDES

Scientists examine numerous causes of school violence. Researchers Daniel Derksen and Victor Strasburger note the abundance of increasingly violent movies, TV shows, and video games targeted toward children and adolescents. They claim these media have changed students' attitudes toward violence and have caused aggressive behaviors. Thomas Jipping of the Free Congress Foundation claims that music is as influential as TV, if not more so. Young fans may internalize the destructive messages of violent music.

Gun control advocates such as participants of the Million Mom March and the National Association of School Resource Officers argue that disputes have always and will always occur at school. They attest it is the ready access to weapons that leads to a deadly escalation of violence.

The Details of Violence

"In most schools," former President Bill Clinton said in July 1998, "it's not the sensational acts of violence, but the smaller acts of aggression, threats, scuffles, and constant back talk that take a terrible toll on the atmosphere of learning, on the morale of teachers, on the attitudes of students."[3]

Some people point to antiauthoritarian educational and parenting methods. These groups lament the breakdown of the traditional nuclear family. Conservative sociologists fear that the increase in single-parent households and broken families results in a lack of parental supervision.

The abuse of alcohol and drugs and the increase of crime in general have also been blamed, particularly in gang-related crime. In his study, *Lost Boys: Why Our Sons Turn Violent and How We Can Save Them*, author James Garbarino has found that in neighborhoods with a high crime rate, schools are

Deadly Lessons

A number of shooting rampages have occurred on U.S. campuses:

- On October 1, 1997, in Pearl, Mississippi, 16-year-old Luke Woodham opened fire at his high school, killing two and wounding seven. Before he went to school that day, he killed his mother.
- On December 1, 1997, in West Paducah, Kentucky, 14-year-old Michael Carneal killed three students at his high school.
- On March 24, 1998, in Jonesboro, Arkansas, 13-year-old Mitchell Johnson and his cousin, 11-year-old Andrew Golden, opened fire on their schoolmates, killing four students and a teacher.
- On May 21, 1998, in Springfield, Oregon, 15-year-old Kip Kinkel shot 25 classmates, two fatally. He also killed his parents.
- On April 20, 1999, in Littleton, Colorado, 18-year-old Eric Harris and 17-year-old Dylan Klebold of Columbine High killed 12 schoolmates and a teacher. They also wounded many others before killing themselves.

likely to experience a high crime rate as well. He notes that an accumulation of risk factors results in violent behaviors. Canadian teen researcher Alan Leschied agrees. He points out that the eruption of violence with a deadly outcome must be seen in the combined context of our society's culture at large, our family culture, and the culture in our schools.

"No child should go to school in fear. ... Schools need to 'take back the controls' and to identify what the local issues are that may be causing fear and anxiety on the part of students and staff. Once the local issues have been identified, school administrators, working with students, teachers, parents and support staff, are able to effect change."[4]

—*National Alliance for Safe Schools*

The Heart of the Controversy

While different groups debate the possible causes of school violence, they also disagree on the best approaches to prevent future acts of aggression. As devastating and frightening as school shootings are, they are isolated and extremely rare. Most students will never hear a gunshot at their school. But these massacres are just the tip of the iceberg. A shooting rampage makes the headlines, but the violence most students encounter at school is more subtle. And

Some U.S. schools have become crime scenes.

most of this violence is committed by kids with very different backgrounds than those of school shooters. The problem of school violence occurs on a variety of levels. Name-calling, bullying, fistfights, threats, theft, and graffiti are only a few examples of aggression that occur across the nation on a daily basis.

Guns or other deadly weapons are not necessary to make verbal and physical confrontations frightening and damaging. Being branded as overweight or homosexual can have very damaging

The Majority and the Minority

The National Alliance for Safe Schools points to the differences between the majority of students and the students who may potentially become violent: "The majority of students are good kids who do their best to play by the rules and to get an education. There is a very small proportion of students who choose to conduct themselves in such a manner as to pose a threat to themselves and to others."[5]

effects on a student's self-esteem. A student who goes to school anxious about the class bully will have trouble concentrating on learning. A teacher who has to deal with disruptive student behavior will have trouble concentrating on teaching. And a school that tolerates any acts of aggression may breed the environment that allows gunfire to erupt.

Deadly school shootings are not the defining moments for U.S. schools. Students with guns are not representative of the nation's student body. Their violent eruptions are the exception, not the rule. The challenge of school violence lies with parents, educators, and policy makers in how they choose to deal with the collective issues: fights, bullying, disruptive behaviors, class cutting, and truancy. If these issues and their causes are addressed, can school violence—and possibly another catastrophic event—be prevented?

Students at the University of Miami pause for a moment of silence
honoring the victims of the Virginia Tech shooting rampage in April 2007.

Bullying has occurred for decades.

WHAT IS SCHOOL VIOLENCE?

School violence includes any verbal, visual, or physical acts that are purposefully demeaning or harmful and violate another person's personal space or civil rights. School violence includes emotional and physical ridicule, bullying, assaults, threats, sexual offenses, gang-related crimes, as well as graffiti and vandalism. Racial slurs, hate-related graffiti, or the hard shove in the hallway are all considered violent acts that involve victimization with varying degrees of seriousness.

Shooting a gun, wielding a knife, or engaging in a fistfight at school clearly constitutes violence and, therefore, unacceptable behavior. The form of violence most students encounter at school, however, may not involve a weapon and may not involve physical violence at all.

On school grounds all over America, hurtful words are used to ostracize students. Taunts or threats on the playground or foul language spray painted on a locker can make school miserable for some students and damage their self-images permanently. None of these examples involve actual physical force or injury. Yet they are all part of what researchers consider school violence.

Forms and Frequency of Bullying

In 2005, approximately 28 percent of students aged 12 to 18 reported being bullied at school. Name-calling was the most common form of bullying. Approximately 19 percent of students had been verbally abused; 15 percent reported being the subject of rumors; 9 percent were pushed, shoved, tripped, or spit upon; 5 percent were threatened with physical harm; and 3 percent reported that their belongings had been damaged on purpose.

Of the students who reported being bullied, more than half had been bullied twice in the six-month period prior to the study, a quarter had been bullied once or twice a month, 11 percent had been bullied once or twice a week, and as many as 8 percent of the students had to deal with bullying on a daily basis.

Vandalism and Graffiti

Vandalism is defined as willfully causing damage or defacing the property of others. Vandalism includes serious acts such as bombing or arson in addition to acts such as kicking in a locker door or tearing up a school library book. The walls and bathroom doors in schools across America are covered with graffiti messages, drawings, and paintings. Though still considered vandalism, graffiti may be a form of artistic expression or nothing other than harmless scribbles.

Often the lines between harmless and hurtful graffiti are very thin. While "John was here" may be a harmless note on a bathroom door, a similar note in a different context may become the touchstone of a turf war among gangs. While "Mary loves Tom" may be a harmless confession of a person's feelings, such a note may prompt extensive ridicule regardless of its original intent.

Many students feel that graffiti is not harmful because it can be cleaned up or painted over. But irreparable damage

"In 2005, 38 percent of middle school students reported seeing hate-related graffiti deliberately using derogatory words or symbols relating to race or ethnicity, religion, disability, gender or sexual orientation."[1]

—*The National Center for Education Statistics*

Graffiti is just one of many forms of school violence.

often is done to an individual student or an entire group of students. Graffiti can be quite hurtful when it is specifically meant to ridicule or express hatred. Hate-related graffiti uses demeaning words or symbols against others due to their ethnicity, religion, disability, or sexual preference. This type of graffiti can be extremely humiliating and demeaning, particularly if it is meant to single out and isolate students. Graffiti has no place at school.

BULLYING

Bullying can take many forms and includes:

❖ name-calling, either in person or spray painted on a locker door;

❖ spreading vicious rumors;

❖ distributing humiliating pictures or information on the Internet;

❖ soliciting certain behavior or items under physical threats;

❖ pushing, shoving, and spitting on people;

❖ repeatedly isolating someone from a group activity;

❖ using physical or verbal abuse to harm, demean, or manipulate someone.

It may be difficult to distinguish bullying from seemingly harmless teasing. Name-calling among elementary school children may be an experiment with acceptable and unacceptable words rather than the attempt to pick on or isolate a particular student. Pushing and shoving may be proof of the age-appropriate lack of control over expressing anger.

By the time students reach middle school, their awareness of the power of words is sophisticated enough to recognize that words can hurt. And hurtful words can be used to ridicule, exclude, or ostracize a fellow student. According to psychologist and professor Peter Sheras, "Boys tend to prefer name-calling, taunts and threats, [while] girls frequently use negative labels and rumor-spreading to ostracize a fellow student and assert their own power."[2]

As with most actions, it is the intent that distinguishes the harmless from harmful use of words. Bullying aims to control, manipulate, demean, ridicule, isolate, or physically harm a fellow student. The bully is usually perceived to be stronger or more powerful. Together with the intent, it is the power imbalance that distinguishes harmful bullying from harmless teasing. In other words, fighting between two equals is not bullying.

Violence toward Teachers

By no means are students the only victims of school violence. The National Center for Education Statistics reports that, "ten percent of teachers in central city schools reported in 2003–2004 that they were threatened with injury by students, compared with 6 percent of teachers in urban fringe schools and 5 percent in rural schools. Five percent of teachers in central city schools were attacked by students, compared with 3 percent of teachers in urban fringe and 2 percent in rural schools."[3] In turn, however, some teachers also bully students. In 2006, the *International Journal of Social Psychiatry* published the results of a study that showed nearly 50 percent of elementary teachers admitted to bullying students.

The popularity of Web sites such as MySpace has made cyber bullying a serious problem. Cyber bullying often goes unnoticed by parents and educators for a long period of time. But it can take on a particularly vicious tone. The aggressor can easily stay anonymous and, therefore, is out of reach of adult supervision and intervention. Internet bullying ranges from name-calling and threats of violence delivered via e-mail to spreading rumors and posting embarrassing pictures.

Bullying can take on a social dimension, when one student or a group of students singles out another with the intent to shun him or her socially. Social abuse often takes the form of exclusion from popular groups or teams. Vicious rumors may be spread about a student so others will avoid that person. Social abuse can also take the form of

Where Violence Occurs

In 2005, 14 percent of students in grades 9 through 12 reported being in fights on school grounds in the previous 12 months. As many as 36 percent of students reported being in fights in general, either on or off school grounds. While not all fights involve weapons, some students report being threatened or injured with a weapon such as a gun, knife, or club. In all surveys pertaining to school violence between 1993 and 2003, at least 7 percent (and sometimes as many as 9 percent) of students reported having been threatened or injured with a weapon. This is not surprising considering that in 2005, 19 percent of students in grades 9 through 12 admitted to carrying a weapon off school grounds, and as many as 6 percent admitted to carrying a weapon on school property.

cultural bullying, when a student is singled out due to his or her racial or ethnic background, religious beliefs, or sexual preference. These types of abuses can create a school climate that systematically abuses students. Over time, these seemingly minor negative experiences build up. This accumulation of negative experiences is what concerns experts.

Sexual Abuse and Physical Violence

The popularity of the Internet among middle and high school students has increased sexually tainted bullying. Sexual bullying can range from name-calling to sexual abuse in varying degrees. While rape is a rather rare occurrence at schools across the United States, sexual gestures, dirty jokes, and name-calling are not.

Not every sexual gesture constitutes bullying or sexual abuse. As with any form of bullying, the intent and power imbalance are what distinguish a serious offense from more minor offenses. Many times, sexual aggression is rooted in ignorance rather than malice. Therefore, it is particularly important to establish and accept boundaries, treat the other person with respect, and accept the ground rules of flirting and dating.

If not eradicated at its roots, teasing, name-calling, threats, shunning, and sexual and social bullying can quickly become physical. There is a wide range of physical violence that includes: playground scuffles, pushing and shoving in the hallway, fistfights, physical or sexual assault, assault with deadly weapons, manslaughter, and murder. A fight or assault off school grounds may often be school related. Many of these fights occur on the way to and from school, just far enough away to escape the school authority's reach.

GANG ACTIVITY

The presence of weapons at school is sometimes related to gang activity. School shooters are often not gang members, however. Typically, gangs are groups of young people that may engage in drug or weapon trafficking and often use violence to defend their turf against a rival gang. Many gangs are ethnically defined, and turf wars may erupt due to racial differences.

Occasionally, gang members are students. But sometimes a school experiences gang-related activity even if none of the students belong to a gang. Outside gangs may infiltrate a school to sell alcohol, drugs, or weapons to nonmembers at a school. Gang activity can be disruptive to the school environment because it may incite fear among the general student population and increase the level of school violence.

ATTITUDES TOWARD SCHOOL VIOLENCE

There is little doubt that gang activity, fights with or without weapons, and physical and sexual abuses have no place in a school or anywhere else. However, less clearly defined occurrences of school violence are often dismissed as normal adolescent

Gangs at School

In 2006, the National Center for Education Statistics reported the following:

"In 2005, some 24 percent of students reported that there were gangs at their schools. Students in urban schools were more likely to report the presence of gangs at their school than suburban students and rural students. ... Hispanic and Black students were more likely than White students to report gangs in their schools in 2005 (38 and 37 percent, respectively, versus 17 percent). This pattern held among students in both urban and suburban schools. Between 2003 and 2005, reports of gangs increased among both Black students (29 versus 37 percent) and White students (14 versus 17 percent). No measurable change was detected in the percentage of Hispanic students reporting the presence of gangs between 2003 and 2005.

"Students in public schools were more likely to report the presence of gangs than were students in private schools regardless of the school's location. This may be due to the selectivity of private schools. In 2005, some 25 percent of students in public schools reported that there were gangs in their schools, compared with 4 percent of students in private schools."[4]

behaviors. Graffiti is often accepted as normal social rebellion. Bullying is often considered a rite of passage. Sexual harassment is excused as harmless sexual experimentation. And social shunning is mistaken for age-appropriate group formation.

Bullying is often subject to ill-informed myths. Some people believe that bullying toughens kids up and is nothing but a phase. Bullies are stereotyped as social outcasts and their victims as nerds. Some believe that all a victim has to do is either ignore the bullying or fight back, and the bullying will stop. Others assume that most bullying is not bullying but harmless teasing instead. Psychologists attest that attitudes that rationalize socially unacceptable behavior underestimate the seriousness of the issue. School violence in all its harmful forms has potentially serious short-term and long-term effects on the individual student, the school as a whole, and society. ⌐

Some students have to navigate gang turf on their way to and from school. Pastor Mike Cummings, right, sometimes accompanies students in Los Angeles, California.

Caitlyn Goldben testifies against Eric Hainstock, who was charged with first-degree murder in the shooting death of principal John Klang.

THE EFFECTS OF SCHOOL VIOLENCE

School violence in all its forms may occur in all age groups from kindergarten to twelfth grade. It is most common in middle and high schools. Adolescents are more socially aware and exhibit greater control over their emotions, words, and actions. Such awareness, control, and knowledge coincides with the increased emotional vulnerability and anxiety typically associated with teenagers. In other words, the time when students have learned to use hurtful behaviors is precisely the time when students are particularly susceptible to such taunts.

Such behaviors do not need to involve physical violence to be damaging. Name-calling alone can have a significant effect on a student's self-esteem, particularly if such name-calling is connected to a person's appearance, racial or ethnic background, religious affiliation, or sexual preference. Most teenagers want to belong. According to psychologist Peter Sheras, "being perceived or perceiving oneself as different can destroy a child's emotional well-being."[1] At the time when teenagers

A Domino Effect

The National Center for Children Exposed to Violence warns, "the topic of school violence is one that affects all of society. Aside from interfering with the learning process, the long range effects of school violence affect us all. Statistically, children who engage in bullying behavior are more likely to become adult criminals. Many children who display violent behavior at school are exposed to violence or abuse outside of school and may be in need of help from adults."[2]

define themselves by their looks and their status within a peer group, being shunned or bullied can have a lasting and damaging effect.

Students who have been repeatedly bullied frequently suffer from decreased self-esteem, truancy, depression, or post-traumatic stress disorder. In extreme cases, a student who is being victimized continuously may become suicidal or retaliate with violence.

"Schools should be places of safety and sanctuary and learning. When that sanctuary is violated, the impact is felt in every American classroom and every American community."[3]

—*President George W. Bush, April 16, 2007, speaking after the Virginia Tech shootings*

DETERIORATING SCHOOL ENVIRONMENTS

Schools are intended to be places of academic and social learning. If students have reason to fear for their safety at school, the school can no longer provide effective academic instruction or offer a training ground for forming positive social relations. Repeated incidents of school violence create an atmosphere of fear and distrust. Students who witness or are part of violence that results in the serious injury or death of a student may begin viewing the entire world as a dangerous place. They might feel that no one can be trusted.

A teacher who continuously deals with disruptive behavior, bullying, or even physical violence spends too much time handling inappropriate confrontations and too little time teaching. Similarly, students engaged in disruptive behavior, bullying, or physical violence, no matter whether they are perpetrators, victims, or bystanders and witnesses, might have difficulty focusing on their studies.

Risk Factors for Violent Behavior

The American Academy of Child and Adolescent Psychiatry lists the following risk factors that may lead to violent behavior in children and adolescents:

- Previous aggressive or violent behavior
- Prior victim of physical abuse and/or sexual abuse
- Exposure to violence in the home and/or community
- Genetic (family heredity) factors
- Exposure to violence in media (television, movies, etc.)
- Use of drugs and/or alcohol
- Presence of firearms in the home
- Stressful family socioeconomic factors (poverty, severe deprivation, marital breakup, single parenting, unemployment, loss of support from extended family)
- Brain damage from head injury

Children who turn to violence often exhibit several of the risk factors and the following behavioral patterns:

- Intense anger
- Frequent loss of temper or quick to anger
- Extreme irritability
- Extreme impulsiveness
- Easily frustrated

This destroys the positive learning environment schools are intended to provide. In turn, this affects a student's readiness and ability to learn. If a student is more concerned about being bullied or attacked at school than about missing class or failing an exam, that student may avoid certain school activities or stop attending school entirely.

Experiencing school violence is extremely stressful, but students who avoid school may not be aware that they do so because they are afraid of being bullied or hurt. Stomachaches, headaches, fevers, and even more serious illnesses may be symptoms of stress disorders that neither the student nor their caretakers are aware of.

Students who stay home may avoid being bullied or hurt, but they may also fall behind academically. Staying at home may also empower the bully. Students who stay home frequently miss the opportunity to interact with peers and make friends. Staying home adds to

Afraid at School

According to the National Center for Education Statistics, "In 2005, approximately 6 percent of students ages 12 to 18 reported that they were afraid of attack or harm at school, and 5 percent reported that they were afraid of attack or harm away from school. ... Consistent with findings from 1999 and 2001, students in 2005 were more likely to report being afraid of an attack at school than away from school."[4]

the sense of isolation the students feel when they are being bullied or ostracized. This vicious cycle is difficult to escape.

THE EFFECTS OF SCHOOL VIOLENCE ON SOCIETY

Aggression at school is often cast off as a phase. Victimization is often kept quiet out of shame,

Avoiding School

Statistics show that in 2005, "some 6 percent of students reported that they had avoided a school activity or one or more places in school in the previous 6 months because of fear of attack or harm; 2 percent of students avoided a school activity, and 4 percent avoided one or more places in school."[5]

embarrassment, or fear of retaliation. And nothing happens to change the school environment. The educational level of a school, a neighborhood, and perhaps an entire community deteriorates.

Schools are an important social training ground. By mixing with their peers, students learn to form relationships and to assert themselves as individuals within a group. If the assertion is verbally or physically abusive, or if group formation is based on the exclusion of certain individuals, students learn unhealthy and socially unacceptable behaviors that will affect them for life. If abusive behavior is tolerated and seemingly successful at school, students will accept and perpetuate such behavior outside of school as well.

Abusive behavior at school may reflect abusive behavior outside the school, either in a particular family, the community, or society at large. Ignoring or downplaying individual incidents of school violence may result in a missed opportunity to improve a particular student's family environment or to detect and combat crime and violence in a specific neighborhood. Overlooking school violence misses an important opportunity to investigate violent tendencies and ways to combat them.

Students, parents, educators, and society should not ignore or underestimate the issue of school violence. Every student, parent, and educator should be aware of potentially violent behavior at school and facilitate early intervention. Students at risk, whether they are victims or aggressors, need to learn to deal with conflict situations in constructive rather than destructive ways. As a first step, it is important to understand where school violence may come from.

Members of Mothers in Charge, a group from Philadelphia, Pennsylvania, who have lost children to violence, hold up antiviolence signs during the Millions More Movement on October 15, 2005, in Washington, D.C.

Kip Kinkel, who killed two fellow students and wounded 25 others at Thurston High School in Springfield, Oregon, as well as murdered his parents, is now serving a life sentence.

WHO COMMITS ACTS OF SCHOOL VIOLENCE?

Not all bullies are stereotypical tough-talking boys from broken homes with bad grades and poor discipline records. As clinical psychologist Peter Sheras explains,

Some bullies earn bad grades in school and have problems with alcohol. Others are popular members of the football team who are on the honor roll. ... Family wealth or status seems to have little effect on whether a child becomes a bully; abusive behavior occurs in children rich and poor. Many children can be kind and friendly on their own, but behave like bullies in a group.[1]

It is impossible to identify a bully by characteristics such as school performance, discipline record, or family economic status. In other words, not only "bad guys" are bullies, and not only "nerds" are their victims. Bullying relationships do not occur only among unpopular students or social outcasts. Indeed, bullies may be male or female, smart or not so smart, rich or poor. Bullies are defined solely by the behaviors they exhibit.

Anger, Aggression, and Bullying

To understand the psychological dynamics of bullying, it is important to understand the differences among anger, aggression, and bullying. Anger is a normal and common human emotion. Every human gets angry once in a while and often with good reason. Anger can be expressed in many different ways. It is quite appropriate to voice one's anger verbally, by stating one's feelings aloud or by writing them down in a journal. Aggression is a potentially inappropriate way to relieve anger. Aggression can be channeled in different ways. Stomping one's feet or punching a pillow are appropriate ways to release aggressive feelings. Bullying, however, is an inappropriate form of aggression.

Bullies, Victims, and Bully-victims

Child psychologist David Elkind describes bullies as children who repeatedly and consistently control their peers by verbal or physical aggression. As opposed to generally aggressive students who may attack any other student, bullies tend to target children who are perceived to be weaker, physically smaller, or younger. Bullies are likely to disregard others' ideas and may refuse to negotiate in play. Contrary to popular belief, bullies often are of average or even above average popularity and do not necessarily suffer from feelings of inadequacy. Some bullies may exhibit above average self-esteem, which may be why they feel entitled to control others.

According to Sheras, it is the victims who often suffer from low self-esteem and a lack of self-confidence. Victims tend to be shy, fearful, or anxious and generally are unable to stand up to aggressive behavior. Instead, they may give in to a bully's demands quickly and repeatedly. Most of a bully's victims are smaller, younger, or physically weaker than the bully. Many victims feel isolated and powerless because they do not have a support group among their peers. They often do not have support away from school either.

Some bullies are victims of violence elsewhere, and some victims of bullying at school become bullies in other situations. These students are categorized as bully-victims, and they share a strong sense of victimization and anger, which, if not channeled appropriately, may find a

Defining Bullies

No child is predestined to become a bully or a victim, neither by their racial, social, or educational background nor by their temperament or a psychiatric condition. Bullies are defined by the behavior they exhibit, not by a psychological predisposition. Some children tend to be shy and quiet, and others enjoy exercising control. But this does not mean that they will automatically become victims or bullies. If channeled, any temperament can be guided toward constructive rather than destructive behavior.

Jacob Rubin, right, was a victim of bullying.

potentially violent outlet. Child researcher T.R. Nansel sees a direct relationship between bullying and the eruption of violence. He states that students involved in bullying, as either the aggressor or the victim, were significantly more likely to exhibit violent behavior at school. Sheras agrees, noting that,

... bully-victims are considered the most potentially violent type—the type to reach for a weapon or join a gang—because their rage is extremely high and their support systems very weak. ... They are angry, in pain and all alone.[2]

School shooters Dylan Klebold, Eric Harris, and Michael Carneal were all victims of repeated bullying before each picked up a gun to shoot others. Bully-victims may see violence as their only way out of a seemingly hopeless situation. In many cases, they may direct their violence against themselves. In fact, many school shootings are intended to be homicide-suicides.

LACK OF SOCIAL SKILLS AND POOR IMPULSE CONTROL

Perhaps the most important psychological aspect of the bully and victim relationship is that neither bullies nor victims have the skills necessary to deal with confrontations. Bullying relationships are often made possible by the inability of the children involved to express and deal with anger, frustration, and fear. Many bullies and victims do not understand their own emotions and what triggers them. They cannot imagine that others may feel the same. Many bullies lack empathy and have not learned to express themselves in ways that do not hurt others. Bullies and victims alike often lack the ability to express and assert themselves with words.

Poor impulse control is often responsible for the eruption of violence. Sometimes impulse control is affected by psychiatric conditions that are beyond the student's control. Mental retardation or mental illnesses such as schizophrenia, mania, or depression can severely curb a student's ability to deal with stress in a constructive manner. For example, school shooter Kip Kinkel was diagnosed with clinical depression before he killed his parents and several of his schoolmates. Less severe psychiatric conditions such as Attention Deficit/Hyperactivity Disorder (ADHD) or Detachment Disorder may be at the root of inappropriate dealings with anger and frustration.

Personality disorders may be directly responsible for a student's repeated aggressive behavior. Not every bully, however, suffers from any of these conditions. According to Raymond Flannery, a nationally recognized expert on violent behavior in youths and its consequences, "It is rare for an act of violence to be caused solely by some medical or psychiatric condition."[3]

FACTORS LEADING TO VIOLENCE

What determines whether a child becomes a bully or a victim? What determines whether a bullying relationship is allowed to continue and escalate into physical violence? Both of these outcomes are affected by forces outside an individual's control. Violence is a contextual phenomenon, and school violence is no exception. This means that sociological factors play as much as if not more of a role in violence than the children involved. No children are born with the

Drinking and Violence

The legal drinking age in the United States is 21. Yet according to the National Center for Education Statistics report, "Indicators of School Crime and Safety: 2006," almost half of all students in grades 9 to 12 surveyed had consumed at least one alcoholic drink in the month prior to the survey. Alcohol and drug abuse is both a function and result of the turmoil and anxiety associated with teenagers. Drug and alcohol abuse can severely affect impulse control and lead to a bullying behavior that escalates into physical violence. This is true whether an individual suffers from the effects of chronic alcohol and drug abuse or from a one-time transgression. The average American boy tries his first drink at age 11; the average American girl tries her first drink at age 13. Americans who develop a drinking problem at some point in their lives usually started drinking regularly at age 16.

The National Institute on Alcohol Abuse and Alcoholism (NIAAA) reports that, "not only may alcohol consumption promote aggressiveness, but victimization may lead to excessive alcohol consumption."[4] In other words, those who drink are more likely to be violent, and those who have suffered violence are more likely to drink.

skill sets necessary to express and assert themselves in healthy and constructive ways. Human behavior and social interaction are learned. Therefore, it is important to investigate the culture of a family, a school, and a society to understand how and why violence may erupt in school. —

The school cafeteria is often a setting for bullying.

New research suggests more families are reclaiming mealtime as family time. The benefit is stronger communication.

The Influence of the Home Environment

arents are often held responsible for their children's conduct, and they are blamed if that conduct is inappropriate. Many people doubt that it is always and only the fault of the parents if a child resorts to aggressive or violent behavior. Child psychologists agree, however, that learning does begin at home.

Children learn how to behave in certain situations and how to interact with other people by watching the examples of others. Children watch how their parents treat each other, how they speak to each other, and whether they treat each other kindly, gently, and with respect. Children also learn by experimenting with their own behaviors and by the reaction their behaviors receive. Children quickly pick up which behavior receives praise and which behavior does not. A child's family culture is a child's first social training ground, and parenting styles define the family's culture.

DEFINITION OF PARENTING STYLES

Child psychologists distinguish between permissive, authoritarian, and authoritative parenting styles and their effects on children. Clinical psychologist Diana Baumrind identified these parenting styles originally. She also identified a fourth style: dismissive parenting, or neglectful parenting.

Protecting the Family Unit

The Universal Declaration of Human Rights protects the family unit: "The family is the natural and fundamental group unit of society and is entitled to protection by society and the State."[1]

This is similar to permissive parenting, but the parent does not care much about the child and is generally not involved in the child's life (but may meet the child's basic needs).

Permissive parents generally attempt to accept and encourage their children's impulses, desires, and actions. Permissive parents do not establish clear limits and avoid parental control and punishments. They allow the child to regulate his or her self. Parent-child conflicts are usually resolved by giving in to the child's desires and demands. Testing boundaries is part of every child's social development by which he or she learns which behaviors are socially acceptable. Children of parents who fail to set and enforce proper limits often push the boundaries of acceptable behavior outside the home as well. It is possible that a child of permissive parents pushes the boundaries of acceptable behavior too far and begins acting out—perhaps even violently.

Authoritarian parents attempt to control their children's conduct, attitudes, and desires by enforcing a clear standard of behavior. Often, the standard of behavior is not defined by the family itself but justified by an outside, higher authority such as strict religious beliefs. The child's personality has to adapt to the often unchangeable set of rules. Authoritarian parents expect obedience and often resort to punishments if the child upsets the rules. Parent-child conflicts usually are resolved by expecting the child to submit to the parents' desires and demands. Authoritarian parents may experience a backlash against their strict rules and disciplinary measures when their children rebel against the set boundaries. A child of authoritarian parents, who do not allow for self-expression, may seek an outlet for anger and frustration.

Authoritative parents attempt to guide their children's behavior by a clear parenting

The Link between Parenting Styles and Conflict Resolution Skills

A study conducted at Johns Hopkins University investigated the relationship between parenting styles and the reaction by adolescents to hypothetical situations that might lead to conflict and violence. Based on the adolescents' descriptions of how their mothers raised them, the mothers were classified as permissive, authoritarian, or authoritative. Presented with several different hypothetical situations that might lead to violent conflict, children of permissive mothers reacted more negatively than the others. The researchers concluded that there is a relationship between parenting styles and an adolescent's ability to deal with conflict.

Which parenting style is most successful in dealing with conflict was not the subject of this study. But the assumption exists that a permissive parenting style does not prepare a child well for conflict, as this style of parenting avoids conflict altogether, and thus does not provide a platform for practice.

policy that not only encourages a child's opinions and desires but sets and enforces a proper standard of behavior. Parent-child conflicts are usually resolved by a verbal give-and-take between parent and child on an issue-by-issue basis. The goal is to teach the child how to be self-assertive while being socially responsible and cooperative. A child of authoritative parents, who seek to find a balance between a child's natural need for self-expression and the limits of such self-expression set by the needs of others, has a good chance to become a healthy and well-adjusted individual.

EFFECTS OF PARENTING STYLES

Only the rare parent follows a pure form of any of these parenting styles. Most parents only lean toward one or the other. It is important to understand that an overly lenient parent and an overly restrictive parent may inadvertently support a child's inappropriate behavior. Reacting to a child's bullying behavior with more and stricter

"Happy families are all alike; every unhappy family is unhappy in its own way."[2]

—*Leo Tolstoy,*
Anna Karenina

rules and punishments may breed the anger and frustration that makes a child with bullying tendencies seek a weaker person to control. This may create the stereotypical bully "with a domineering parent who punishes frequently and praises rarely."[3] However, indulging a child and showing too much understanding for a child's bullying behavior may increase what child psychologists have termed narcissistic, or selfish, tendencies. The child then fails to understand that one's actions can cause pain to others. This may create the stereotypical bully from a privileged background whose parents cater to their child's every need, yet, as Sheras notes, "rarely make an effort to curb her aggressive behavior."[4]

> "To put the world in order, we must first put the nation in order; to put the nation in order, we must put the family in order; to put the family in order, we must cultivate our personal life; and to cultivate our personal life, we must first set our hearts right."[5]
>
> —*Confucius*

Parenting is most successful if parents are involved in their children's upbringing and if they approach their children with calm reasoning when setting limits and enforcing them. The authoritative parenting style is successful because it demonstrates and exemplifies constructive conflict resolution. Authoritative parents aim to explain the reasons

Reactive Attachment Disorder

Abuse and neglect may be responsible for certain personality disorders, which in turn may be responsible for some instances of youth violence. A person suffering from Reactive Attachment Disorder is unable to establish caring relationships with others. A person suffering from Oppositional Defiant Disorder shows constant defiance toward authority figures and disregards rules of conduct. A person suffering from Conduct Disorder often resorts to violence when showing defiance toward authority.

behind the boundaries they set and react calmly and with reason if the child fails to abide by those rules. Rather than reacting impulsively by shouting or imposing harsh punishments, such as spanking or hitting, authoritative parents attempt to demonstrate nonviolent ways of conflict resolution. Quite simply, if parents want their children to stop hitting or taunting their peers, such behavior cannot be tolerated at home from anyone: not the child, the sibling, or the parents.

DOMESTIC ABUSE AND NEGLECT

The majority of child psychologists agree that physical violence in a child's home contributes to a child's potentially violent misconduct at school. Domestic abuse includes physical, sexual, and verbal abuse of a spouse, children, or other family members. Abuse may occur in homes of all social, racial, and cultural backgrounds. Children may

Legislation has been proposed that would make it illegal to market or sell devices, such as spanking paddles, to be used solely for hitting and whipping children.

be abused by a parent or another family member, even siblings. Being subject to or just witnessing such abuse breeds feelings of rage, paired with a sense of helplessness and hopelessness. A child who is victimized at home may try to release his or her feelings of anger and despair by victimizing another weaker child.

Child maltreatment, consisting of neglect and child abuse, may range from a lack of parental supervision to a failure to provide for a child's physical and emotional needs. A child who is left to his or her own devices and the child who comes home to an empty refrigerator and a place without heat may show symptoms of neglect. Neither receives the attention nor the care he or she deserves. Neglect may occur in the two-parent, two-income household where child rearing is left to a series of caregivers. It may occur as well in a low-income, single-parent household where time constraints eliminate constructive parenting. Children from all backgrounds, if left with little or no parental supervision, may act out violently to receive the attention they need and to offset their sense of loneliness.

Sociological Changes

The middle-class family of the 1950s with a stay-at-home mother, a working father, and biological children has provided the idealized norm for families to follow. This idealized family as presented in television shows evoked ideas of safety, cordiality, and compassion. The nurturing two-parent family was considered to be the basis of American society.

Sociological developments, such as higher divorce rates, have increased the number of single-parent households. Growing financial demands have increased not only the number of families with two working parents but the number of children raised by nonfamily members. These sociological changes have been used often to lament the loss of family values and morality. The American Family Association (AFA) regrets the loss of such traditional values. Groups such as the AFA have been accused of not acknowledging positive developments brought about by this change. Today's family often includes a father who is not only concerned with breadwinning but is also actively involved in the child rearing process.

Changing family values suggest that a more varied notion of what constitutes an American family must be accepted. Yet, these changed values do not suggest that a single-family household, a broken home, or a family with two working parents relying on hired child

What Is a Family?

Families come in all shapes and sizes. The traditional family is a married couple with children. It does not include grandparents, aunts, uncles, nieces, nephews, or other members of the extended family. It is the family that became typical in Western civilizations in the nineteenth century. Its demise has been lamented since the 1950s, at the very time it was celebrated most in TV shows such as *Father Knows Best*, *Leave It to Beaver*, and *The Adventures of Ozzie and Harriet*.

In 1960, almost half of all American households had a married mother and father with biological children. Today, only a quarter of American households fit that description. The 1960s were also a period of social and political change. In the 1970s, the baby boomers were marrying later or not at all. The decline in the traditional family unit is also due to an aging population. Today, there are many more empty-nest families and single households that lost one partner to death.

care constitute a training ground for maladjusted children. Unhealthy home environments are defined by how children are raised, not by who raises them. A single mother or father, a gay or lesbian couple, a hired nanny, two working parents, or a stay-at-home mother may or may not raise their children equally well. Unsuccessful parenting styles, and even parental neglect or child abuse, can and do occur in traditional nuclear families. School shooters Eric Harris, Kip Kinkel, and others came from two-parent, middle-class families. ⌒

The cast of the TV series Leave It to Beaver *portrayed an idyllic American
family in the late 1950s and early 1960s.*

On average, children in the United States watch more than
40 hours of television each week.

MEDIA'S INFLUENCE: ARE
YOU WHAT YOU WATCH?

Children of all ages spend so much time
in front of the television and playing
video games that child psychologist James Steyer
calls television "The Other Parent."[1] In his study on

the effect of the media on children, Steyer cites a University of Maryland study that reports children spend an average of 17 hours a week with their parents as opposed to an average of more than 40 hours a week in front of the television. It appears evident that television is an integral and important part of every child's life. Many do not consider this a positive development.

NEGATIVE EFFECTS OF MEDIA EXPOSURE

The arguments against television and video games are plentiful. Continuously watching a fast succession of images, particularly during commercials, shortens a person's attention span. Constantly watching television or playing video games is antisocial and can create lonely children with poor social skills. It can stifle individual creativity and create children who can no longer occupy themselves and are dependent on constant entertainment.

Author Madeline Levine points out that, in the context of school violence, media violence "encourages aggression,

"Television has replaced all other institutions as the single most powerful transmitter of cultural values."[2]

—*Madeline Levine,*
Viewing Violence

desensitization, and pessimism in our children."[3]
The contemporary media landscape has become so
diverse and seemingly uncontrollable that television
and the media as a whole are considered harmful.
Numerous studies have been conducted about the
relationship between violence on television and
violent behavior. Studies by the U.S. Surgeon
General (1972), the National Institute of Mental
Health (1982), the American Psychiatric Association
(1992), and the American Medical Association
(1996) all mention the issue of aggression. These
studies suggest that watching televised aggression will
increase later violent actions and that such behavior
can create a long-term pattern. The dangerous effect
of media violence spans television shows and movies,
cartoons and video games, and includes the news
media and a sensationalized portrayal of crime
and war.

IMITATING VIOLENCE

Stating a direct correlation between media
violence and violent behavior in children and
adolescents is largely based on the assumption
that children learn by imitation. Often cited is an
experiment conducted by Albert Bandura in 1961.

Children who had first seen an adult hitting a doll were more likely to later mimic the violence. Their reaction was also a more violent reaction than that of children who had not seen any behavior model at all. This is in direct contrast to children who had seen an adult modeling nonviolent responses to the doll. Children who had seen a positive model reacted with the least violence. Bandura concluded that observing violent behaviors in adults might lead children to believe that such behavior is acceptable, thus weakening the natural inhibitions to act out aggressions.

While this experiment helped establish the principle that children learn by imitation, it is not well established that children cannot and will not distinguish between media violence and violence in real life. Hitting an inanimate object such as a doll is not the same as

Violence on Television

The Kaiser Family Foundation reports that almost two out of three television programs contain violence, and fewer than 5 percent contain a positive nonviolent message. Sixty-nine percent of television shows directed at children and 57 percent of television shows directed at adults contain violence. Researchers were most concerned with "sinister combat violence" shown on Saturday morning television. Violence is central to the story line of many Saturday morning cartoons that feature a hero using extreme violence to defeat an equally violent villain.

hitting one's classmate. Hitting inanimate objects such as a pillow or a punching ball is considered a valid method of releasing aggression.

Children often imitate scenes they have first seen in television, movies, or video games. In most cases, this goes no further than playacting and role-playing, which are generally accepted as valid ways to learn how to deal with fear, anger, frustration, aggression, violence, and death.

An extreme example of today's display of violence is the so-called first-person-shooter games such as *Doom*, a video game focused on violence and shooting. Dave Grossman is a retired lieutenant colonel in the U.S. Army and a professor of military science at Arkansas State University. He argues that video games play to the more violent aspects of human nature and cites the fact that the video game industry advertises such games as a way to "kill your friends guilt-free."[4] Considering the U.S. Marine Corps uses *Doom* "to train their combat fire teams in tactics and to rehearse combat actions of killing," it appears that the interactive quality of these video games allows the players to improve their real-life aim.[5] But does playing a game such as *Doom* alter a person's real-life behaviors?

Research indicates that violent video games influence the decisions and inhibitions of young viewers.

The increase of violence in the media has not necessarily coincided with an increase of violence among youths in general or in schools in particular. The National Center for Education Statistics reports that,

> between 1992 and 2004, the victimization rates for students ages 12 [to] 18 generally declined both at school and away

**Violence in
Western Countries**

The U.S. Department of
Justice cites that compared
to the United States, there
are fewer incidents of violent crime in general and
school violence in par-
ticular in other Western
countries.

*from school; this pattern held for
the total crime rate as well as for
thefts, violent crimes, and serious
violent crimes.*[6]

The 1990s showed decreasing
crime rates among adolescents
despite increased exposure to
violent images in the media.
This is not to say that media
violence is harmless and has
no effect on children. Some
research has found that TV violence is as effective
in producing aggressive behavior in kids as smoking
is in producing lung cancer. The founder and
former president of the Entertainment Software
Association admits that there is evidence that
media violence "may lead to more aggressive play."[7]
However, such play lacks the intent to injure, which
is the psychological definition of aggression. Media
violence, however, does not turn children into
killers. Other factors lead some children and not
others to act out the violence they see.

School shooters Michael Carneal, Dylan
Klebold, and Eric Harris may have been fans of

aggressive movies and video games. However, they also had been subject to repeated bullying by their schoolmates. They perfectly fit the profile of the bully-victim. The movies they watched and the games they played did not make them the killers they ended up to be. But their interest in these movies and games may have been incited by other risk factors in their personal lives and may have lessened their inhibitions to kill.

However, as author Karen Sternheimer notes, presuming that the media are "responsible for creating hatred and resentment in youth" fails to recognize that our media culture's violent expressions

---

Does Media Violence Create Killers?

Some theories argue that some of the more horrid incidents of school violence may have been modeled on or influenced by violent television shows, movies, and video games. Before shooting three of his schoolmates at Heath High School in Kentucky, in 1997, Michael Carneal had reportedly watched the 1995 movie *The Basketball Diaries* and remarked how cool it would be to go on a shooting rampage similar to the one depicted in a dream sequence in the movie. Although Carneal had never practiced with a real gun, his aim was remarkable, which was attributed to the hours he had spent playing violent video games.

The Columbine High shooting also shows eerie similarities to the same dream scene in *The Basketball Diaries* in which the main character, dressed in a black trench coat, shoots several students in his high school. Eric Harris and Dylan Klebold, the Columbine High shooters, also were avid players of *Doom* and fans of the Oliver Stone movie *Natural Born Killers*, which satirizes the glorification of violence on television.

are "deeply rooted in social realities."[8] *The Basketball Diaries* deals with the real-life experience of drug addiction, *Natural Born Killers* addresses issues of child abuse, and a video game such as *Doom* draws heavily on images of war. Some groups argue that the problem with our media culture is not so much that children see violence on television, but that what they see may, in fact, be a representation of the underlying realities of society. ⌐

The Oliver Stone film Natural Born Killers *has been blamed for lessening the violent inhibitions of people such as Michael Freeman, seen here during his murder trial.*

Elvis Presley was one of the first music icons accused of influencing youth behavior in negative ways.

THE INFLUENCE OF YOUTH CULTURE

While children are exposed to more and varied media, the fear of what continued exposure to new media and pop culture might do to young, impressionable minds is not a new concept.

Karen Sternheimer is a sociologist from the University of Southern California. She shows that the potential negative effects of new media and pop culture have been the subject of age-old discussions. Plato was concerned about the influence of Greek tragedies on children because the dramas could incite passion. In early nineteenth-century England, penny theaters and cheap novels were feared to have a bad influence on working-class boys. Penny theaters were cheap and attracted the lower classes. The gatherings of young men, often poor and without much hope for a better future in newly industrialized England, were considered threatening. In the 1940s and 1950s in the United States, comic books were considered dangerous due to their graphic images of violence. The music of the 1950s and 1960s and Elvis Presley swinging his hips to rock and roll were considered sexually offensive. Today, it is the often-violent lyrics of shock rock and rap music that are considered unfit for young minds.

Sternheimer argues that the fear of pop culture masks a fear of social change. The fear of penny theaters and cheap novels masked a fear of the growing literacy of the working class. The widespread claim that the violence in comic books

"Most kids deserve the respect their parents wanted when they were kids: to be able to consume bits of pop culture and decide on their own whether it's poetry, entertainment or junk. There is a lapse in parental logic that goes from 'I don't get it' to 'It must be evil,' and from that to 'It makes kids evil.'"[1]

—*Richard Corliss,*
Bang—You're Dead

was responsible for many negative influences upon the younger generation in the 1940s, 1950s, and 1960s failed to recognize that comic book violence was an expression of and rebellion against the violence in American society at the time. McCarthyism and an extremely violent movement against communism, and the physical violence that came with wars fought in Europe, Korea, and Vietnam, characterized the mid-twentieth century. Elvis Presley's music made traditionally black music accessible to white teenagers during a time when segregation controlled American society. His music allowed the two cultures to approach each other.

The fear of the influence of pop culture on children is the fear of influences that are beyond the control of a parent or an educator. It is the fear incorporated in any generational shift, namely the fear that the next generation will not carry on the values of its elders. Social change is brought about by a gradual shift in values. The older generation often worries that the younger generation will adapt the wrong values. The voices against today's pop culture claim that the younger generation is materialistic, oversexed, violent, and alienated from both family and society.

Do Marilyn Manson, Shock Rock, and the Goth Movement Provoke Violence?

In her discussion of music and its influence on children and adolescents, Sternheimer disagrees with the voices that blame media in general and music in particular for the sense of alienation and its potentially violent expression. Marilyn Manson is a shock rocker whose lyrics are full of images of murder, suicide, and satanic rituals. In the wake of the Columbine shooting, Manson was often blamed for glorifying violence and thus leading his young fans to commit murder and suicide. Serious attempts were made to ban his music from public broadcasting and to severely limit access to his concerts.

Marilyn Manson's music is often associated with Goth, a youth subculture that has been falsely accused of promoting anarchy,

"There is a sound basis for concluding that some popular music can help lead some young people to violence."[2]

—*Thomas Jipping,*
Diagnosing the
Cultural Virus

violence, nihilism, atheism, and Satanism. But Goth is neither a political nor a philosophical movement. It draws its fascination with the darker side of human nature from the culture of the Gothic novel and horror movies of the early twentieth century rather than Satanism. Eric Harris and Dylan Klebold were loosely associated with members of a group of students who called themselves the Trenchcoat Mafia, a group who mostly wore black and Goth clothing and accessories. This was enough to make the Goth movement a scapegoat for the Columbine massacre, seemingly proving that it advocated very wrong values.

Experts such as Sternheimer would argue that wearing extreme makeup and clothes, donning provocative symbols often of a religious nature, and listening to music with violent lyrics will not automatically lead to sexual promiscuity and violence. Adolescence is a time of separation and rebellion against an individual's first peer group—the family. In search of a unique personal and social

"I'm a poster boy for fear. Because I represent what everyone is afraid of, because I say and do whatever I want."[3]

—*Marilyn Manson responding to Michael Moore's question about why he was held responsible for the shootings at Columbine High in Bowling for Columbine* identity, adolescents often choose to associate with a peer group different from their family, sometimes precisely because it is considered extreme. Because popular youth culture is confusing and different from what parents know and understand, it is often feared and demonized.

Addressing thought-provoking issues and social problems such as racism, war, and hatred in music is not the same as condoning and glorifying them. Sternheimer argues that many Marilyn Manson fans are drawn to his music

Goth

Goth subculture draws heavily from the themes and imagery of nineteenth-century Gothic literature, which combined elements of horror and romance. Prevalent themes of Gothic literature included a rebellion against the religious establishment, particularly Catholicism and its practices of the Spanish Inquisition, a melodramatic view of love and death, and a preoccupation with the dark nature of man expressed by the fascination with monsters, vampires, and werewolves.

Today's Goth subculture is defined by a stress on individualism and a tolerance toward any and all individual lifestyles. This is in part responsible for the fact that Goth subculture cannot easily be defined as a movement with a particular philosophy. Goth has been considered atheistic, although it embraces religious themes and symbolism. Goth has more to do with a shared fashion sense, a romantic mood, and a certain taste in music than it does with a social, political, or religious agenda. Although many see Goth as a reaction against social conservatism, much like the hippie movement of the 1960s or the punks of the 1970s, the Goth subculture does not necessarily promote social change. Its explosive power stems more from its aesthetic symbols and postures, which are often considered offensive to mainstream culture.

U.S. rock star Marilyn Manson has been blamed for encouraging school violence.

because it deals with their life experience. She notes, "Manson attempts to speak to kids who feel like outcasts."[4] It is not Marilyn Manson's music or his lyrics that create social outcasts who might express their alienation violently. But those who feel like outcasts are often drawn to his music.

Does Rap Music Provoke Violence?

Rap music also has been considered as a source of youth violence. Unlike Goth music and shock rock, which are expressions of a predominantly white middle-class youth culture, rap is primarily an urban black music genre. Rap portrays life of minority youths in an urban setting. Rap themes include poverty, substance abuse, gangs, rape, murder, and the sense of alienation from mainstream America. Attitudes about rap range from the belief that it is a valid social commentary to the concept that the music contributes to hatred of women and a glorification of crime and violence. Thomas Jipping works with The Free Congress Foundation, a conservative group in Washington, D.C. He cites the American Medical Association when he claims that music has a greater influence on young minds than television. He argues that rap music contributes to a culture of aggression by celebrating violence. Jipping believes the debate is not a matter of generational differences

"The obvious causes of social violence—economic inequality, racism, and racial profiling—are all but ignored when the focus is on the music of (minority) youth."[5]

—Michael Eric Dyson, Testimony before the Senate Commerce, Science and Transportation Committee, September 11, 2000 in taste but a matter of harm to society. Some studies do find links between violent lyrics and violent thoughts and behaviors.

Others argue that rapping about violence is not the same as condoning it. Listening to music portraying the reality of substance abuse, rape, and murder is not the same as shooting up heroin, violating women, and killing gang members. Becky Tatum is an assistant professor of criminal justice at Georgia State University. She claims that criticisms of rap music are "based on stereotypes against African Americans."[6] Such stereotypes criminalize the musicians and their fans rather than addressing the social realities that may have led to the crime and violence depicted in their songs. Criminalizing youth culture fails to recognize that any subculture may react to real and imminent societal problems and dangers rather than cause them. ⌐

*In London, England, rapper RhymeFest met with the head of the
Conservative Party to discuss violent rap lyrics.*

Students leave for summer vacation.

THE INFLUENCE OF
SOCIAL FACTORS

he Constitutional Rights Foundation is
a nonprofit, nonpartisan, community-
based organization that publishes online lesson
plans pertaining to civic issues. It reports that the
occurrences of school violence "mirror the trends of

violence in our larger society."[1] Therefore, in order to understand school violence, it is important to understand violence in general.

The Challenges of a Multicultural Society

Violence in general, and school violence in particular, is contextual: it is a function of social realities and the attitudes toward them. The United States is not a homogenous society. American society is made up of people from various ethnic, racial, social, religious, educational, and financial backgrounds. The United States is truly a multicultural and multiethnic society.

So many people from different backgrounds living together can result in culture clashes when differences are seen as threatening. Humans tend to gather in groups that define themselves by common characteristics and set themselves apart from and at odds with groups and individuals who do not share these characteristics. People judge

Leading Cause of Death

In the article "Violent Behavior," health care author Sydney Younger-man-Cole notes the serious effects of hostility: "Violence causes more injuries and deaths in children, teenagers, and young adults than infectious disease, cancer, or birth defects. Homicide, suicide, and violent injury are the leading causes of death in children. Violence related to guns is the leading cause of death of children and teenagers in the United States. Approximately 3,500 teenagers are murdered every year and 150,000 are arrested for violent crimes."[2]

Hate Crimes

Based on data collected by the Federal Bureau of Investigation (FBI), an estimated 7,163 incidents of violent hate crimes occurred nationwide in 2005. Hate crimes included an African-American teenager who was beaten up by white teenagers while driving to school, a swastika spray-painted on a synagogue, a gay man attacked by heterosexuals, and the use of racial epithets at women wearing traditional Islamic clothing. Almost two-thirds of the attackers and almost half of the victims of hate crimes were under the age of 24.

other lifestyles and often resent them simply because those lifestyles are different and they do not understand them. Such attitudes create stereotypes. Minorities are often subject to stereotypes based on little more than how their ethnic or cultural background differs from the background of the majority. Hate crimes are often motivated by stereotypes and preconceptions that have little to do with reality.

DOES POVERTY LEAD TO VIOLENCE?

While the United States is a truly multicultural and multiethnic society, it is not a truly equal society. The idea that there is a right way and a wrong way to live finds its expression in the excesses of hate crimes, as well as in other more subtle economic and social realities. Educator James Banks from Washington University states,

Groups of color have experienced three major problems in becoming citizens of the United States. First, they were denied legal citizenship by laws. Second, when legal barriers to citizenship were eliminated, they were often denied educational experiences that would enable them to attain the cultural and language characteristics needed to function effectively in the mainstream society. Third, they were often denied the opportunity to fully participate in mainstream society even when they attained these characteristics because of racial discrimination.[3]

Due to this history, minorities are more likely to be poor than whites. Census studies have shown that the poverty rate among African Americans and Hispanic Americans is higher than that among white and Asian Americans.

A relationship between poverty and violence can be established not because poor people are violent, or because violent people are poor, but because "poverty compounds other problems."[4] Poverty means not having adequate funds to provide

"Everyone has the right to a standard of living adequate for the health and well-being of himself and of his family, including food, clothing, housing and medical care and necessary social services, and the right to security in the event of unemployment, sickness, disability, widowhood, old age or other lack of livelihood in circumstances beyond his control."[5]

—*Universal Declaration of Human Rights, Article 25*

The accumulated negative effects of living in poverty can lead to school violence.

food, clothing, and shelter. Such a situation creates stress factors that may immediately or indirectly lead to violence. People may steal, rob, or hurt someone for sheer survival in order to get food or clothing or money to buy food or clothing. All of these pressures of survival and negative experiences can accumulate to put a youth at risk for violent behavior.

Poverty affects health care and education. For example, parents working several jobs may not have time for adequate parental supervision of their children. This may lead to children performing poorly at school because they cut class altogether or do not do their homework. Due to a lack of money for doctor visits or for medication, children may be sick frequently. This may lead to frequent absences from school, which in turn may lead to poor performance at school. Alternatively, if parents are often ill, they may lose their jobs. A sense of hopelessness may develop. Such frustration and anger may lead to alcohol and substance abuse, which leads to poor impulse control, which may lead to violence. Poverty may lead to a culture that considers crime and violence as a means to make money. Many members of street gangs see crime as their only way out of poverty.

GANGS AND YOUTH VIOLENCE

Malcolm Klein, former director of the Social Science Research Institute at the University of Southern California and professor emeritus, is one of the most well-known gang researchers in the United States. He defines a street gang as "any enduring street-oriented youth group for which

Poverty Rates

According to the U.S. Census Bureau, while the official U.S. poverty rate in 2005 was 12.6 percent, the poverty rate was 24.9 percent among blacks and 21.8 percent among Hispanics. Among whites, the poverty rate was 8.3 percent. Children under the age of 18 are more often affected by poverty at a rate of 17.6 percent as opposed to 11.1 percent of adults.

illegal activity is part of its identity."[6] The potential for criminal activity separates a street gang from any other youth groups. Klein states that while criminal gang activity has increased in recent years, "most gang members come together for identity, for belonging, for excitement, for what they think is going to be protection" against crime and violence in their neighborhood.[7] Gang formation may be as simple as loosely knit groups of individuals hanging out together. More formal gang organizations have a leader or a ruling council. These gang members wear gang colors, gang identifiers, and use a formal gang name that is recognized by other gang members and rival gangs. An important aspect of the attraction of gangs is that they are youth groups, unsupervised by adults, and self–determined. They define themselves as a subculture and

The Origins of Gangs

Gangs originally started in inner-city environments, in part out of economic necessity, as ill-conceived means to get out of the ghetto by engaging in criminal activity. The shock value of the gang culture has allowed the phenomenon to spill into American suburbs.

While race and ethnicity are often major factors in the original gang formation, "gang clothing, language, and music have been seized on for commercial exploitation [...] and diffused worldwide."[8] Gang colors and listening to gangsta rap have been separated from their original economic and racial factors and become popular the world over.

do so in part by delinquent acts, some of which may be violent. That is also what can make them attractive to young people who do not live in typical poverty-stricken or crime-ridden neighborhoods.

Violent Communities

The National Center for Education Statistics reports that schools in urban areas of high levels of crime are more likely to report violent and serious crime than schools in neighborhoods with low levels of crime, suggesting that the violence in communities has a direct effect on children.

Therefore, schools all over the United States, even if they are not in traditional gang territory, may be vulnerable to gang activity. Organized gangs engaging in criminal activity may try to extend their markets and influence by approaching even younger students in schools within their immediate neighborhoods. Children not living in violent or impoverished neighborhoods may adapt gang subculture along with its tough and potentially violent postures.

ARE GUNS AND VIOLENCE RELATED?

According to Josh Sugarman, executive director and founder of the Violence Policy Center in Washington, D.C., "studies reveal that urban gang membership is a predictor of handgun carrying. The same studies reveal an increase in white suburban adolescent gun carrying."[9] While gangs are engaged in weapons trade, not all guns are bought or sold by or to criminals. Many young people have access to guns in their homes.

The American Academy of Pediatrics and other child care experts, as well as many nonprofit organizations such as The Brady Campaign to Prevent Gun Violence or the Coalition to Stop Gun Violence, see a direct relationship between the ready availability of guns in U.S. homes and the threat posed to American youth by gun violence. American children are at a considerably higher risk of being shot, accidentally as well as purposefully, than children in other countries. The one common difference between the United States and countries with less violent crime is the ready availability of guns in the United States.

Many children who bring guns or other weapons to school do so for protection. The mere presence of weapons at school helps perpetuate an intimidating and threatening atmosphere. In addition, by carrying a weapon at school, one is tempted to use it. Thus a student taking a weapon to school for protection may end up contributing to the violence.

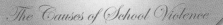

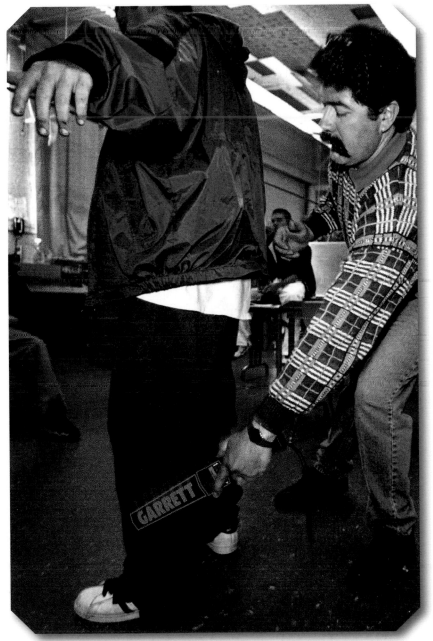

Using airport-style metal detectors, a security officer checks students for weapons in Hollywood, California.

*A trooper carries an assault rifle on the Virginia Tech campus following the
April 2007 deadly shootings in Blacksburg, Virginia.*

CAN SCHOOL VIOLENCE
BE PREVENTED?

t seems self-evident that weapons should
be banned from schools. Some school
districts have imposed strict gun and weapon control
policies. It is much more likely that a conflict among
students will escalate into physical violence and result

in injury if weapons are involved. But the increased security necessary to enforce such a ban may involve undesirable procedures and side effects. Stationing uniformed security officers around a school and installing security cameras or metal detectors to ensure that the ban is not broken may increase the atmosphere of fear and distrust. In turn, this environment might spur more violence. Critics of such measures note that a lockdown mentality better suits a prison than an educational institution meant to foster creativity and curiosity. Enforcing a weapons ban by a zero-tolerance policy brings with it an entire set of problematic issues of its own. A student disregarding the ban is subject to serious consequences such as suspension or expulsion.

"Everyone has the right to education. ... Education shall be directed to the full development of the human personality and to the strengthening of respect for human rights and fundamental free-doms. It shall promote understanding, tolerance and friendship among all nations, racial or religious groups."[1]

—*Universal Declaration of Human Rights, Article 26*

ZERO TOLERANCE

Zero-tolerance policies rest on two assumptions. The first assumption is that the fear of punishment is a deterrent. The

"Mass shootings have come to define our nation. Today's shooting at Virginia Tech—the largest mass shooting in U.S. history—is only the latest in a continuing series over the past two decades. These tragedies are the inevitable result of the ease with which the firepower necessary to slaughter dozens of innocents can be obtained. We allow virtually anyone the means to turn almost any venue into a battlefield. In the wake of these shootings, too many routinely search for any reason for the tragedy except for the most obvious —the easy access to increasingly lethal firearms that make mass killings possible."[2]

—Josh Sugarman,
Violence Policy Center,
April 16, 2007, in
relation to the massacre
at Virginia Tech in
Blacksburg, Virginia

second assumption is that crime in general, and school violence in particular, is committed by repeat offenders who show clear warning signs. Yet, school violence does not presuppose a bad disciplinary record, and a bad disciplinary record is not a clear indication for school violence. Zero-tolerance policies may lead to the scapegoating of certain groups of people and to criminalizing students for minor offenses.

Minor offenses may lead to unfair or unnecessary suspension or expulsion from school. However, even arguably deserved suspension or expulsion from school does not solve the disciplinary problem of a particular student. It simply removes the student from school grounds. Releasing a student with disciplinary problems to unsupervised and unstructured

The debate over gun rights is part of the school violence controversy.

time away from school may support and increase
the disciplinary problem. Children may spend their
time in less constructive, potentially harmful ways.

REGULATION OF MEDIA VIOLENCE

Regulating media violence may function as a tool
to prevent school violence. Such regulation may
include requests for a universal and standardized

rating system that is legally binding to alert parents and educators of content that is potentially harmful to minors. The current rating system for movies, TV shows, and video games is self-imposed by the media. It is not standardized or supervised by an independent group.

Media regulation may also include bills such as the Media Marketing Accountability Act of 2001, proposed by Democratic Senator Joe Lieberman. The bill was meant to prevent the music,

---

A Right to Bear Arms

The Second Amendment to the U.S. Constitution guarantees the right of the people to keep and bear arms. Whether one believes that gun control is constitutional rests on the interpretation of this amendment. More specifically, does the Second Amendment guarantee the right to keep and bear arms only as a member of a militia? Or does it guarantee a broad and unrestricted right to keep and bear arms to the individual?

The United States no longer has a militia. Today's equivalent, the National Guard, has limited membership and uses a government-supplied arsenal of weapons rather than privately owned weapons. Thus, gun control issues do not affect the effectiveness of a militia. Therefore, the issue is only whether private ownership is guaranteed under this amendment and whether a particular gun control law violates this right. For example, do age restrictions, background checks, stricter gun-registration procedures, and more and stricter gun safety features infringe upon this right? Do these restrictions unduly empower the government to decide who can buy a gun? Or do they help ensure the safety of children and adolescents by making sure that those with a questionable background (criminal history, a history of mental health problems, or substance abuse) or exposed to certain risk factors cannot be in possession of a gun?

game, and movie industries from marketing violent products to children.

Opponents such as Danny Goldberg, a representative of the music business, argued that such regulation amounts to government censorship. This legislation essentially decides which products will be available by severely curbing the economic viability of certain products. Considering that such legislation may also target youth culture, the government would essentially decide what is and what is not considered acceptable cultural expression.

Regulation may also affect coverage of violence by the news media. The Rocky Mountain Media Watch favors such regulation. It argues that sensational news coverage of school violence, for example, has contributed to a national hysteria falsely assuming that schools are unsafe. Lawrence Grossman, former president of NBC News and PBS, opposes censorship of news coverage. He and other opponents cite the First Amendment and argue that censorship in any shape or form is unconstitutional. While criticism is a constructive force of change, censorship by the government is potentially dangerous and may lead to prosecuting people for their viewpoints or ideas.

Dress Codes

Censoring what students wear to school by establishing dress codes is aimed at banning gang insignia and avoiding evidence of social inequality. Some experts advocate this approach. They argue that if everyone wears the same types of clothing at school, peer pressure to wear a particularly desired brand of clothing disappears, and with it, the importance of a student's economic background. Social and economic inequality, often reasons for conflict, become invisible. Affiliation with a certain gang, also often at the root of school violence, becomes invisible as well.

Opponents of dress codes argue that censoring what a student wears at school stifles creativity and individual expression, and it is ineffective in masking social disadvantages or gang affiliations. With or without dress codes, students usually know whether a classmate belongs to a gang or comes from an affluent background. Dress codes are ineffective in preventing potentially violent conflict.

Tolerance and Conflict Resolution

Measures combating the roots of school violence rather than just its symptoms may be more effective, particularly in the long run. Many schools have introduced a social curriculum designed to change the school environment by establishing positive models of conflict resolution. Such programs aim to:

❖ reduce prejudice and increase tolerance among students.

❖ improve relations among individual students and entire groups by actively promoting and teaching nonviolent conflict resolution.

❖ support educator development in these constructive approaches to school violence.

A Summit on School Violence

On October 10, 2006, President Bush convened a summit on school violence. In several panel discussions, school officials, Parent Teacher Association (PTA) representatives, members of President Bush's cabinet, and law enforcement officers came up with a basic tried-and-true response: Open the channels of communication and get parents, school teachers, students, police, and community representatives to work together.

Such programs may include skill building for students and training for teachers, counselors, and support staff. Such programs teach students and teachers to recognize potential conflict situations and to deal with them constructively. Students are taught to handle anger, frustration, and fear in assertive yet nonviolent and nonthreatening ways.

Teachers are taught to handle conflict situations and disruptive behavior in equally nonviolent, nonthreatening, and nonpunitive ways. This may involve programs aimed at teaching the opponents to handle the conflict by themselves or with mediators. This may involve programs that focus on the school environment alone and programs that include the student environment at home and in the community. Such violence-prevention programs work with communities, businesses, and churches. The goal is to bring nonviolent conflict resolution to the neighborhood as a whole, thus combating violence as a societal problem.

There will always be differences in appearance, as well as social, financial, racial, religious, and educational backgrounds. People who live, work, and go to school together may not always like each other. Teaching constructive and nonviolent ways to deal with conflict helps promote tolerance and understanding—and perhaps lessens the causes of school violence.

Skill-building programs, such as this one led by Annica Trotter, work to create constructive environments.

TIMELINE

1940s–1950s

In the United States, comic books are considered dangerous due to their graphic images of violence.

1960

Almost half of all U.S. households have a married mother and father with biological children.

1998

On May 21, Kip Kinkel shoots 25 classmates, killing two. He also kills his parents.

1999

On April 20 in Littleton, Colorado, Eric Harris and Dylan Klebold kill 12 schoolmates, a teacher, and themselves.

1961

Experiments show that children who had first seen an adult hitting a doll were more likely to react with similar violence when frustrated.

1994

The Educate America Act proclaims that by 2000, U.S. schools will offer a learning environment free of weapons, drugs, and violence.

2001

The Media Marketing Accountability Act is proposed to prevent the music, game, and movie industry from marketing violent products to children.

2002

Bowling for Columbine, Michael Moore's documentary about the Columbine, Colorado, shootings, is released.

TIMELINE

2003–2004

During the school year, 96 percent of high schools and 94 percent of middle schools report violent incidents of crime.

2005

Reports note that hate-related graffiti is witnessed by 38 percent of middle school students.

2006

On October 10, President Bush convenes a summit on school violence.

2007

On April 16, Seung-Hui Cho, a 23-year-old student, shoots and kills 33 people on the Virginia Tech campus, including himself.

2005

Approximately 24 percent of students report gang presence at their schools.

2006

Almost half of all students in grades 9 to 12 surveyed have had at least one alcoholic drink in the month prior to the survey.

2007

In early November, Finland witnesses its first school shooting.

ESSENTIAL FACTS

AT ISSUE

While access to weapons is clearly a contributing factor to physical violence and may lead to particularly serious injury or even death, the question whether gun control is constitutional is subject to debate. Most schools have established a ban on weapons. Some schools enforce such a ban with zero-tolerance policies. Other schools attempt to combat school violence with conflict resolution programs and other programs introducing increased security.

Despite sensationalist reports on violent eruptions on U.S. campuses, American schools have not experienced an increase in violence over the past decade. However, school violence includes a wide variety of inappropriate behaviors such as emotional and physical ridicule, bullying, assaults, threats, sexual offenses, gang-related crimes, as well as graffiti and vandalism. School violence in all its shapes and forms can have serious psychological implications on an individual, severely damaging self-esteem, possibly leading to a variety of post-traumatic stress disorders.

❖ School violence is influenced by factors such as family culture, school environment, and societal factors.

❖ A physically or emotionally unhealthy home environment is one of several risk factors.

❖ A community with violence and gang activity is another, as is prior engagement in a bully/victim relationship at school.

❖ Alcohol and substance abuse may lead to poor impulse control, which in turn may lead to violence.

❖ Ready access to guns and other weapons is an environmental factor that may lead to incidents of physical school violence.

❖ Media violence (television, movies, music, and video games) is often blamed as contributing to school violence.

CRITICAL DATES

1961

Albert Bandura's experiment showed that children who had first seen an adult hitting a doll were more likely to mimic the action themselves later.

2001

The Media Marketing Accountability Act of 2001 was proposed to prevent the music, game, and movie industries from marketing violent products to children.

2006

President Bush convened a summit on school violence to open the channels of communication among parents, teachers, students, and the community.

QUOTES

"Schools should be places of safety and sanctuary and learning. When that sanctuary is violated, the impact is felt in every American classroom and every American community."—*President George W. Bush, April 16, 2007, speaking after the Virginia Tech shootings*

"In most schools, it's not the sensational acts of violence, but the smaller acts of aggression, threats, scuffles, and constant back talk that take a terrible toll on the atmosphere of learning, on the morale of teachers, on the attitudes of students."—*President Bill Clinton*

ADDITIONAL RESOURCES

SELECT BIBLIOGRAPHY

Bowling for Columbine. Michael Moore. United Artists, 2002.

Flannery, Raymond. *Preventing Youth Violence*. New York: Continuum Publishing, 1999.

Levine, Madeline, Ph.D. *Viewing Violence: How Media Affects Your Child's and Adolescent's Development*. New York: Doubleday, 1996.

National Center for Education Statistics, Indicators of School Crime and Safety: 2006. <http://nces.ed.gov/programs/crimeindicators/index.asp#top>.

National Youth Violence Prevention Resource Center. *Youth Firearm-Related Violence Fact Sheet*. <http://www.safeyouth.org/scripts/facts/firearm.asp>.

Sheras, Peter. *Your Child: Bully or Victim? Understanding and Ending School Yard Tyranny*. New York: Skylight Press, 2002.

Sternheimer, Karen. *It's Not the Media: The Truth About Pop Culture's Influence on Children*. Boulder, CO: Westview Press, 2003.

Steyer, James P. *The Other Parent: The Inside Story of the Media's Effect on Our Children*. New York: Atria Books, 2002.

FURTHER READING

Garbarino, James, and Ellen deLara. *And Words Can Hurt Forever: How to Protect Adolescents from Bullying, Harassment, and Emotional Violence*. New York: The Free Press, 2002.

Gerdes, Louise, ed. *Media Violence: Opposing Viewpoints*. San Diego, CA: Greenhaven Press, 2004.

Haerens, Margaret. *Gun Violence: Opposing Viewpoints*. New York: Greenhaven Press, 2006.

Web Links

To learn more about the causes of school violence, visit ABDO Publishing Company on the World Wide Web at **www.abdopublishing.com**. Web sites about the causes of school violence are featured on our Book Links page. These links are routinely monitored and updated to provide the most current information available.

For More Information

For more information on this subject, contact or visit the following organizations.

Center for the Prevention of School Violence
4112 Pleasant Valley Road, Suite 214, Raleigh, NC 27612
919-789-5580
www.ncdjjdp.org/cpsv/
Contact the center for resources on preventing school violence and promoting positive youth development.

Constitutional Rights Foundation
601 South Kingsley Drive, Los Angeles, CA 90005
213-487-5590
www.crf-usa.org/violence/links.html
A group dedicated to educating young people on becoming active and responsible citizens, the foundation provides links to numerous resources on school violence, its causes, and preventions.

National Crime Prevention Council
2345 Crystal Drive, Fifth Floor, Arlington, VA 22202
202-466-6272
www.ncpc.org/topics/school-safety
Find resources and tips to keep schools safe, identify strategies to prevent violence, and communicate more effectively within your community.

GLOSSARY

abuse
> Treating another person in a harmful way; the abuse can be physical, emotional, sexual, or social.

adolescent
> A young person who has undergone puberty but has not yet reached adulthood.

aggression
> Hostile or destructive behavior; forceful action with the intent to dominate.

alienation
> The emotional detachment, disassociation, and isolation that is often felt by adolescents.

assertiveness
> The ability to express one's feelings, opinions, and desires in an honest yet respectful way that does not insult or infringe upon the rights of others.

bullying
> Intentionally tormenting another person by verbal or physical harassment with the intent to ridicule, manipulate, or isolate.

censorship
> Examining books, film, music, games, and other material and removing or suppressing what is seen as morally, ethically, or politically objectionable, dangerous, or offensive.

conflict
> A serious disagreement or argument over seemingly incompatible opinions or interests.

conflict resolution
> The process during which a dispute is put to rest or solved.

desensitize
> To render less sensitive and responsive.

hate crime
> A crime motivated by prejudice against a social group; the prejudice may be based on race, ethnicity, gender, age, religion, sexual preference, disability, or appearance.

impulse control
> The ability to control one's emotions and the involuntary reactions they cause.

nihilism
> Negative disbelief.

nuclear family
> A family consisting of two parents and their children, but not grandparents, aunts, or uncles.

poverty
> A lack of sufficient funds to take care of basic needs such as food, shelter, clothing, health care, and education.

prejudice
> An opinion formed prematurely without knowledge or experience; the prejudice may go as far as irrational suspicion or even hatred of a person or group of persons based on race, ethnicity, gender, age, religion, sexual preference, disability, or appearance.

punitive
> Inflicting or imposing punishment.

stereotype
> A conventional, oversimplified, and generalized opinion about a person or a group of persons.

substance abuse
> Indulging in and depending on addictive substances such as alcohol or narcotics.

truancy
> Repeated absence from school without permission or good reason.

zero tolerance
> Enforcing a rule or law without granting exceptions; originally a policy used in law-enforcement, zero-tolerance policies have been used to enforce weapon-free and drug-free schools on some American campuses.

SOURCE NOTES

Chapter 1. How Much Violence Occurs?
1. 103rd Congress of the United States of America. Goals 2000: Educate America Act, Section 102, National Educational Goals. 25 Jan. 1994. <http://www.ed.gov/legislationGOALS2000/TheAct/sec102.html>.
2. Constitutional Rights Foundation. Web Lessons: School Violence. <http: www.crf-usa.org/violence/school.html>.
3. Bill Clinton. "School Violence: Are American Schools Safe?" *CQ Researcher*, 9 Oct. 1998. 892.
4. National Alliance for Safe Schools. History. <http://www.safeschools.org/history.htm>.
5. Ibid.

Chapter 2. What Is School Violence?
1. National Center for Education Statistics. Indicators of School Crime and Safety 2006. Indicator 10: Student Reports of Being Called Hate Related Words and Seeing Hate Related Graffiti. <http://nces.ed.gov/programs/crimeindicators/ind_10.asp>.
2. Peter Sheras. *Your Child: Bully or Victim? Understanding and Ending School Yard Tyranny*. New York: Skylight Press, 2002. 40–41.
3. National Center for Education Statistics. Indicators of School Crime and Safety 2006. Executive Summary. <http://nces.ed.gov/programs/crimeindicators/index.asp>.
4. National Center for Education Statistics. Indicators of School Crime and Safety 2006. Indicator 8: Students' Reports of Gangs at School. <http://nces.ed.gov/programs/crimeindicators/ind_08.asp>.

Chapter 3. The Effects of School Violence
1. Peter Sheras. *Your Child: Bully or Victim? Understanding and Ending School Yard Tyranny*. New York, NY: Skylight Press, 2002. 44.
2. The National Center for Children Exposed to Violence. "School Violence." <http://www.nccev.org/violence/school.html>.
3. George W. Bush. "President Bush Shocked, Saddened by Shootings at Virginia Tech." 16 Apr. 2007. The White House Web site. 28 Nov. 2007 <http://www.whitehouse.gov/news/releases/2007/04/20070416–2.html>.
4. National Center for Education Statistics. Indicators of School Crime and Safety 2006. Indicator 16: Student's Perception of

Personal Safety at School. <http://nces.ed.gov/programs/crimeindicators/ind_16.asp>.

5. Ibid.

Chapter 4. Who Commits Acts of School Violence?

1. Peter Sheras. *Your Child: Bully or Victim? Understanding and Ending School Yard Tyranny*. New York: Skylight Press, 2002. 49.

2. Ibid. 50.

3. Raymond Flannery. *Preventing Youth Violence*. New York: Continuum Publishing, 1999. 34.

4. The National Institute on Alcohol Abuse and Alcoholism. *Alcohol Alert*, No 38, Oct. 1997. <http://pubs.niaaa.nih.gov/publications/aa38.htm>.

Chapter 5. The Influence of the Home Environment

1. *Universal Declaration of Human Rights*. Article 16.3. 10 Dec. 1948. 28 Nov. 2007 <http://www.un.org/Overview/rights.html>.

2. Leo Tolstoy. *Anna Karenina*. Trans. Helen Edmundson. London: Nick Hern Books, 1994. n. pag.

3. Peter Sheras. *Your Child: Bully or Victim? Understanding and Ending School Yard Tyranny*. New York, NY: Skylight Press, 2002. 50.

4. Ibid.

5. Confucius. From *Analects*. Conservative Forum Web site. 28 Nov. 2007. < http://www.conservativeforum.org/authquot.asp?ID=205>.

Chapter 6. Media's Influence: Are You What You Watch?

1. James P. Steyer. *The Other Parent*. New York: Atria Books, 2002.

2. Madeline Levine. *Viewing Violence*. New York, NY: Doubleday, 1996. 15.

3. Ibid. xiv.

4. Dave Grossman. "Violent Video Games Encourage Violent Behavior." Louise Gerdes, ed. *Media Violence: Opposing Viewpoints*. San Diego, CA: Greenhaven Press, 2004. 58–65.

5. Ibid.

6. National Center for Education Statistics. Indicators of School Crime and Safety 2006. Indicator 2: Incidents of Victimization at School and Away from School. <http://nces.ed.gov/programs/crimeindicators/ind_2.asp>.

SOURCE NOTES CONTINUED

7. Douglas Lowenstein. "Violent Video Games Do Not Encourage Violent Behavior." Louise Gerdes, ed. *Media Violence: Opposing Viewpoints*. San Diego, CA: Greenhaven Press, 2004. 66–74.
8. Karen Sternheimer. *It's Not the Media*. Boulder, CO: Westview Press, 2003. 144.

Chapter 7. The Influence of Youth Culture
1. Richard Corliss. "Bang, You're Dead." *Time*, 3 May 1999. 50.
2. Thomas Jipping. "Diagnosing the Cultural Virus." Louise Gerdes, ed. *Media Violence: Opposing Viewpoints*. San Diego, CA: Greenhaven Press, 2004. 75.
3. *Bowling for Columbine*. Dir. by Michael Moore. United Artists, 2002.
4. Karen Sternheimer. *It's Not the Media*. Boulder, CO: Westview Press, 2003. 131
5. Becky Tatum. "Studies Have Not Established a Link Between Rap Music and Youth Violence." Louise Gerdes, ed. *Media Violence: Opposing Viewpoints*. San Diego, CA: Greenhaven Press, 2004. 89.
6. Ibid. 84.

Chapter 8. The Influence of Social Factors
1. Constitutional Rights Foundation. The Challenge of School Violence. Web Lesson. <http://www.crf-usa.org/violence/school html>.
2. Sydney Youngerman-Cole. "Violent Behavior." Revolution Health. 16 Jan. 2007. 28 Nov. 2007 <http://www.revolutionhealth.com/articles/?id=viobh>.
3. James A. Banks. *Educating Citizens in a Multicultural Society*. Teachers College Press, 1997. xi.
4. Raymond B. Flannery. *Preventing Youth Violence*. New York: Continuum Press, 1999. 36.
5. *Universal Declaration of Human Rights*. Article 25. 10 Dec. 1948. 28 Nov. 2007 <http://www.un.org/Overview/rights.html>.
6. Marshall Allen. "Q&A With a Gang Expert." 28 Sep. 2004. *Enough is Enough, A Look at Gangs in Southern California*. Long Beach, CA: Long Beach Press Telegram, 1 July 2007.
7. Ibid.

8. John Hagedorn. "Gangs." Karen Christianson and David Levinson, Eds. *The Encyclopedia of Community*. Sage Publications. <http://gangresearch.net/Archives/hagedorn/gangcom.html> 517-522.

9. Josh Sugarman. "Youth Gun Violence Is a Serious Problem," Margaret Haerens, ed. *Gun Violence: Opposing Viewpoints*. New York: Greenhaven Press, 2006. 37–43.

Chapter 9. Can School Violence Be Prevented?

1. *Universal Declaration of Human Rights*. Article 26. 10 Dec. 1948. 28 Nov. 2007 <http://www.un.org/Overview/rights.html>.

2. Josh Sugarman. "Violence Policy Center Statement on Virginia Tech Shooting, Deadliest in U.S. History." Violence Policy Center. 16 Apr. 2007. 28 Nov. 2007 < http://www.vpc.org/press/0704vatech.htm>.

INDEX

ABOUT THE AUTHOR

Helga Schier, a native of Germany, holds a Ph.D. in language and literature. Schier has written and published on many different subjects ranging from art to education to history to language to literature to social studies. She writes with a passion for history, a love of the present, and excitement for the future. Schier lives in Santa Monica, California.

PHOTO CREDITS

Charles Dharapak/AP Images, cover, 3, 86; Rogelio Solis/AP Images, 6, 11; Wilfredo Lee/AP Images, 13, 98 (bottom); Maurice Ambler/Picture Post/Getty Images, 14; Max Whittaker/Getty Images, 17, 98 (top); Reed Saxon/AP Images, 25, 99; Andy Manis, Pool/AP Images, 26; Brendan Smialowski/Getty Images, 33; Pool/AP Images, 34, 96 (bottom); Noah Berger/AP Images, 38; Daniel Hulshizer/AP Images, 43; The Indianapolis Star, Sam Riche/AP Images, 44; The Tribune-Review, Michael Henninger/AP Images, 51; AP Images, 55, 66, 96 (top); Jupiterimages/AP Images, 56; Carlos Osorio/AP Images, 61, 97; Ed Nessen/AP Images, 65; Vadim Ghirda/AP Images, 72; Yui Mok, PA/AP Images, 75; Chris Gardner/AP Images, 76; Charles Rex Arbogast/AP Images, 80; John Capple/Getty Images, 85; Jacquelyn Martin/AP Images, 89; Jeff Roberson/AP Images, 95